GET HOOKED!

A Bedtime Book for the Fisherman

by
Dave Rees

Copyright © Dave Rees 2015
This book is sold subject to the condition that it shall not, by way of trade or otherwise, be lent, resold, hired out, or otherwise circulated without the publisher's prior consent in any form of binding or cover other than that in which it is published and without a similar condition including this condition being imposed on the subsequent publisher.
The moral right of Dave Rees has been asserted.
ISBN-13: 978-1519793232
ISBN-10: 1519793235

To my loving wife Jean
and
Miffy, much loved and missed.

CONTENTS

1. IF ONLY 1
2. THE TAKE 5
3. RIVERSIDE REFLECTIONS 10
4. FISHING AND THINKING 15
5. FORMIDABLE FLAVOURED FLIES 19
6. ELEVENTH HOUR ENCOUNTER 24
7. A PISCEAN POINT OF VIEW 30
8. BACK TO SCHOOL 34
9. MONTANA MAN 42
10. FISHING CAN HARM YOUR HEALTH 47
11. TACKLE SHOP TEMPTRESS 51
12. ONE LAST CAST AND A BOY 56
13. BEND IN THE RIVER 62
14. THE BRIDGE 68
15. HELLO THE GOLDEN YEARS 72

ACKNOWLEDGMENTS

With thanks to Fly Fishing and Fly Tying Magazine, who first published most of the stories and poems featured in this book.

1. IF ONLY

Yes, the big IF. We've all said it sometime or other and never more so than

in this book where if only I'd taken the trouble —whoops! I've done it again.

If only I'd twigged what was happening
On the last day of March this year
When a queue at the Post Office stretched for miles
Well, I thought it seemed a bit queer
I later found out they were anglers
Paying their licence fee
Because if you forgot and then got caught
You'd be joining The Club — with me!

DAVE REES

If only I hadn't stepped backwards
And trod on my brand new rod
It was intended to be a four-piece job
But now I've got rather a lot
It fits easily into my pocket
Next to my penknife and phone
But by the time I've put it together
It's almost time to go home

If only I'd taken more notice
Of the sign on the fishery gate
It warned you of overhead power lines
When casting a – oops! Too late
Well, I'd never seen triple-forked lightening before
And it promised one helluva time
As it arced from pylon to fly rod
Then made its way down my line

If only we'd spotted this damn great bull
Before crossing the field to the lake
We'd have worn some different colours
Yes! Red was a big mistake!
So with fingers crossed we retreated
All the way back to the gate
Hoping like hell it was colour-blind
And it wasn't calling its mate

GET HOOKED!

If only I'd kept a grip on myself
When the blonde arrived at the lake
She started to sunbathe unnervingly close
And I missed three consecutive takes
I should have asked her to go somewhere else
And honour Club Rules to the letter
Instead I moved up the bank a bit
To where I could see her much better

If only I hadn't stopped fishing
When the skies turned stormy and red
And I went back home to the missus
Who was dozing and still in bed
I slipped quietly in beside her
And whispered the weather was bad
And to think my husband's gone fishing, she said
He must be stark raving mad

If only I hadn't dropped my priest
When taking it out of my pocket
It headed straight for my fly box
Despite my attempts to stop it
It landed just like a missile
After striking my left big toe
And that's when my open fly box
Fired all its flies in one go

DAVE REES

If only I'd been less hasty
When assembling my rod today
And realised I'd missed out two of the rings
And the reel was on the wrong way
I doggedly carried on casting
Things couldn't get any worse
'Till I noticed a sign which clearly said
All anglers must book in first

If only I'd started before it got dark
To stow all my tackle away
My battery was flat and the car wouldn't start
It definitely wasn't my day
I freewheeled and pushed for over an hour
To the lodge where I'd last seen my mates
Then my troublesome car started just like a dream
But some wally had padlocked the gates

If only I hadn't been so naive
When we danced at the Fly Fishers Ball
She was gorgeous and French with a lakeside chateau
Oh, yeah! She had it all!
I only wish that she'd made it quite clear
When I accepted her invite to France
That she only wanted to learn how to fish
As for anything else - not a chance!

2. THE TAKE

He had a decision to make. He could reach out a hand and receive in return unconditional love, or try to avoid those deep brown eyes that were anxiously searching his face. Which was it going to be?

"The one on the left is Winston. The one on the right is Ben. Beautiful aren't they?"

I'd been joined at the lake by someone I'd seen on odd occasions before and she was looking across to the opposite bank where two Labradors sprawled in the sun, relaxed but fully alert. They kept looking in our direction as though listening to what we said and gave the occasional deep-throated *woof* to let us know they were there. I remarked that they'd come from nowhere and seemed to be on their own. "I've only recently joined the angling club," I explained, "so I haven't seen them before. Do you know who their owners are?"

She nodded and faintly smiled. "Well, up until fairly recently they belonged to my husband Geoff who was a professional trainer of sporting dogs but sadly he died last year. We often appeared at the County Shows displaying retrieval techniques but all I do now is keep them in shape with the odd demonstration round here. So I'm happy to say they belong to me and I'm glad of their company. I'm Mary Cattell by the way."

"Please call me George," I said. I asked what she meant by retrieval techniques and she seemed quite keen to explain.

"Once caught, it's a way of playing your fish. You can forget any fears about breaking strains, or applying far too much pressure. You simply need a retrieval machine that does all the worrying for you." She nodded proudly at Winston and Ben. "There's two of them over there. Retrieval machines on four legs!"

She laughed at my puzzled face. "Look. I'll demonstrate what I mean. And as this isn't the County Show I'll try and use real live fish, not dummies. Now, as we were only out for a walk do you mind if I borrow your rod? I'll do my best not to break it."

*

Ten minutes later I sat by the lake watching her cast my floating line between an avenue of willow trees. With expertise, smoothness and grace, she put my casting to shame. Although sitting quite still on the grassy bank, the dogs were like coiled up springs. Then, all of a sudden, they sprang to their feet trembling and all alert. A splash had caught their attention and Mary was into a fish. They were whining with sheer excitement at those challenging moments ahead, moments of leaping and heart-stopping swirls as the fish tried hard to break free. Then Mary called out to one of the dogs whose judgement was crucial in getting *The Take* just right. Timing was everything. Winston was first to go, gliding calmly across the water to where the fish was thrashing about. Then, pausing for just a few seconds in a fleeting moment of calm, his jaws closed gently around its girth and *The Take* was successfully made. Mary relaxed her hold and Winston headed for home. With the fish held firm in his velvet-soft mouth Winston returned to the bank and clambered up on the grassy slope and dropped it at Mary's feet. There wasn't a single mark on it. Mary carefully removed the barbless hook and returned the fish to the lake and the dogs settled down again, still keeping a watchful eye. Mary sat down beside me praising the work that Winston had done.

"There, George! That's how it's done," she beamed but within minutes was up on her feet again when the rod tip started to twitch and the rod bent into an arch. The fly we tied on earlier on must have been a good choice. This time it was Ben's turn to shine, sliding gently into the water at Mary's simple command. "It feels like a brownie," Mary called out loosening off some line. "It's certainly gone down deep."

Ben paddled hard to get to the spot then looked back at Mary for help. She pointed and called out again. "Just there! Right where you are!" Then whoosh! Up came the fish near Ben's waiting mouth and *The Take* was over in seconds. Minutes later it was brought to the bank and placed before Mary's feet. She made a point of praising them both with biscuits she kept in a pocket. For the moment their job was done.

She asked if I'd like to swap places. "I'm sure there's still some fish to be had and you can try out the dogs as well."

As much as I loved to play a fish, it was an offer I couldn't refuse and within minutes the dogs were working again and we landed another two fish. Once more they were placed unmarked by our feet and this time the praises were mine. I asked if I could give them more biscuits for a job really well done. In a strange sort of way I was beginning to feel that I and the dogs felt quite natural together and that Mary was watching me closely.

*

A pathway led back to Mary's house and my car that was parked closeby and while Mary made us a welcome drink we stood and talked for a while. I found myself thinking about the dogs and how good it would feel if they were running around my own empty house back at home. It wouldn't seem quite so empty now that I lived alone, and they'd be very good company.

Mary was watching me closely and must have seen the look in my eyes as my thoughts drifted around. Then she beckoned me round the back of the house where a dog came running to greet us. He was another retriever like Winston and Ben and was a rescue dog, she explained. She said that his name was Blackie who'd also been trained to catch fish. She looked me solemnly in the face.

"I wouldn't normally do this," she said, "but I think the man and the moment is right. Is there any chance you could give Blackie a home and plenty of TLC? My sister's coming to live with me and she's bringing two dogs of her own. I don't really have room for more."

I was flattered she'd put her trust in me but I'd not owned a dog before. I needed a little more time to think and after chatting a while to Blackie arranged to call back next day. Blackie just sat and stared at me when he saw me going away. The hope in his eyes had faded and the look on his face said it all.

*

I knew next day when I called back again I would leave a much poorer man. There'd be dog food to buy, perhaps vet bills to pay, and other expenses like that. More than that he'd be mine for a lifetime which was quite a commitment to make. In return I'd be richer in other ways...guaranteed unconditional love and life shared with a very good friend.

I was feeling a touch apprehensive as we made our way down to the lake. Blackie was wearing an anxious look knowing this was our first time out. If I had any doubts that I'd done the right thing I needed only to glance down at my side where Blackie kept looking up at me with anxious and hopeful eyes. They seemed to be asking only one thing.

"We're going to be okay, aren't we?"

I patted his warm and silky head and said, "We're gonna be fine, just you see."

3. RIVERSIDE REFLECTIONS

We've all done it. Made a mistake about something in life and wished we could put it right. This man about town goes further that. And all it took was a minute or two after looking down from a bridge.

How did it all begin, this fly fishing thing that I do? It all began on a midsummer day at a pub by the riverside.

It had been a glorious start to June and I was happy to sit with a pie and a pint watching the world go by. I nodded to Bob a regular who was walking back to his car. He walked rather stiffly and awkwardly but with determination written all over his face. I would have said he was approaching eighty, and something, no doubt arthritis, had already taken its toll. He started to take things out of his car and I guessed from the net and a few other things he had an afternoon's fishing planned. My attention immediately waned. I'd tried to take an interest in fishing before but from things that I'd read and conversations I'd heard it didn't appeal somehow. No, fishing wasn't for me.

But with no inclination to go back to work I followed him up to the bridge where he carefully climbed over a rickety stile leading down to the river below. Curious, I watched for a while. He was stealth on legs and on reaching the river's edge he stopped and stared at the water for quite some time. Motionless. Just like you see herons do.

I began to think....what happens next? Where's all the gear that fisherman have? He appeared to have nothing except waist-high wellies, a small canvas bag, and a net slung over one shoulder. His rod, all of 9ft long and just like a wand, looked far too fragile to use. Then, much to my surprise and growing concern, this elderly arthritic gentleman slipped slowly into the water with barely a movement or sound. I was intrigued because I could see something was different now. His body language had changed. Gone was the bent-over figure I'd followed up to the bridge. Now he was standing tall and proud at one with his sport and nature. He waded carefully out to the middle where he turned and faced downstream.

I took more than a passing interest as he pulled line off a murmuring wheel. It was the clickety-click that caught my ear, a sound that I'd grow to love. It was a sound that announced you were ready to start and make that very first cast. It was a kind of musical prelude to the challenge that lay ahead.

Bob was at home now, his weathered right arm rising and falling in a regular motion as the powerful thrust of his slender rod punched more and more fly line over his head in a delicate, graceful movement. With effortless grace he continued to feed out line, backwards and forwards in lengthening loops until its tip came down on the water a considerable distance away. I was to find out later that on the end of that line was a much finer one called a tippet, and on the end of that tippet was tied a fly that Bob, with arthritic fingers, had lovingly made the evening before from feathers and fur and things. His quarry was wild brown trout.

I found myself totally mesmerised. There was more to this sport than I thought. I was glued to that bridge for a good half-hour watching the skill and grace of it all. Bob changed his position several times, tirelessly casting to different spots for something to fancy his fly. Then, suddenly, his rod was a quivering wand and all hell broke loose at the end of his line confirming a take was made. A careless fish had taken his fly and he was into something big. I could see it was a powerful fish, a beauty, bending Bob's rod in a graceful arc as he skilfully played his catch. I found myself down there with him, breathing hard, my heart up in my mouth. Take it steady now, Bob, I was urging. We don't want to lose it now!

It took him nearly ten minutes to slowly wind in his line, unable to use too much pressure in case that very fine tippet broke - and both fish and fly would be lost. But Bob's years of experience showed and, with all the line wound back on the reel, his catch was safe in the net. I watched him examine the fish, remove his fly, then return it back to the river, and imagined how many times he'd caught that fish and returned it every time. Perhaps they'd become good friends! When he waved at me with a thumbs-up sign the look on his face said it all. He had seen it, caught it, and touched it, and I'd watched his contact with nature with an envy I never expected. As I watched from the bridge on that warm sunny day I wanted that experience, too.

I'd been completely wrong about fishing. It wasn't a case of sitting around or drowning worms like some folks say, and just had to give it a try. So I purposely called in at the pub next day in the hope that Bob would be there. I wanted to ask him about his kind of fishing and what should I do to begin. He looked at me over his pint and suggested I pulled up a chair.

"Fly fishing, that's what it's called and it's a wonderful gift from God. It's a pity you've left it so late to start so you'll just have to go twice as often to make up for the years you've missed."

He chuckled over his logic and after painting a picture of what his fishing was like he didn't say much for a while. It seemed something was on his mind.

"Tell you what," he announced. "If you really are serious and anxious to learn I have a suggestion to make. I'll take you fishing one day a week. You buy me lunch in return. You can also borrow some old gear of mine until you know you would like your own. And that will cost you a beer each time! What do you think about that?"

It didn't take much thought at all. Private tuition with gear thrown in. I considered myself very lucky.

"Yes. It's a deal," I replied. "When can we start?"

Luckily, happily (and thanks, Bob, for teaching me) that's how it all began. And forty years on there might be a need to pass on that knowledge again. I can see a few lads looking down from the bridge all curious to know what I'm doing.

4. FISHING AND THINKING

Fishing and thinking is what life's all about and makes for a strenuous day.
Our pondering thinker is at it again watching the world go by.

I like to think about things
When I'm fishing down at the lake
Simple things that drift through my mind
Like... when did I last have a take?
Was it some weeks ago, perhaps even months
When that rainbow fell to my fly?
I'm blowed if I can remember now
But it feels like a lifetime's gone by.

DAVE REES

I like to think about life
When I'm down at the lake on my tod
And those shiny bright blue dragonfly things
Perch on the end of my rod.
I really don't like to disturb them
As we doze in the afternoon sun,
While dozens of trout have gone for my fly
And I've bloomin' well missed every one.

Next to pass by are Mum and Dad swan
Out for a cruise on the lake
All the family are with them of course
Cruising along in their wake.
But I know damn well when I get my first take
They'll change course and start heading my way
And I'll shout and tell them to take themselves off!
Well, something like that anyway.

I like to think about things
When I'm down at the lake on my tod
Like why do I stand too close to things
When yielding a twelve foot rod?
I hadn't realised how close I was
To this fly-eating sycamore tree.
Then – twang! Too late. Another fly lost
It happens quite frequently.

GET HOOKED!

I suspect that tree's been a nuisance
And a challenge for many a year
And it didn't take long to mess up again.
Using words I cannot say here
The tree's becoming a problem as well
With its metal hooks everywhere
It's beginning to show on the radar screens
At the airport not far from here.

In my quieter moments of fishing
Like when sheltering from the rain
I do a bit of a stock take
To top up my flybox again.
But why do I always get carried away
And order a Bargain Lot
And end up having too many flies
For the empty spaces I've got?

And how can I spend a penny
When there's a lady angler nearby?
She'll only guess where I'm going
Especially as I'm a guy
So I'll try and act like a gentleman
And just casually saunter by
With hands in my pockets and whistling aloud
Whilst gazing up at the sky.

But she must have heard me howling
When I found a suitable spot
Where I failed to see the notice which said
Danger. Electric Fence. Guess what!
I was still tingling and very embarrassed
When I passed her on the way back
But she said I shouldn't worry too much
I wasn't the first to do that.

Right now there are hundreds of swallows
Zooming all over the place
They've just got back from their holidays
And are desperate to find a space
I find them a bloomin' nuisance
Always chasing after my fly
And I'm praying like hell I don't catch one
As catch-and- release rules apply.

Well, I guess I can tell when you've had enough
So I'm tempted to call it a day
I bet you've enjoyed it really
Seeing what happens all day
And if ever you'd like to join me again
To see us experts at play.
Well, all you need do is give me a shout
And book another magical day.

5. FORMIDABLE FLAVOURED FLIES

Our man has a well kept secret when it comes to tying his flies, but along comes Jim to spoil all that – at least so it seems for a while.

In all the years I'd been fishing I'd never done such a thing. There I was at the lakeside but my lunchbox was still at home. Back at the house my doting wife would be shaking her head in despair after spotting my precious lunchbox left behind on the windowsill.

My lunch at the lake was always the same – succulent juicy chicken thighs cooked the previous night. They were also my secret weapon in my weekly pursuit of fish having read somewhere that my quarry had senses of smell and taste. I thought it through for a while. What would attract them the most? What would turn a dry bushy fly into a seemingly tasty morsel? I put my thinking cap on. It occurred to me then that I *always* caught fish after eating my chicken thigh lunch. Did my fingers, greasy with chicken fat, leave a taste on the fly I'd tied on? Was it that that was driving them crazy? I had to give it a try and on my very next visit I put my theory to the test. It worked like a fisherman's dream!

So now when I finish my chicken thigh lunch I tie on a large bushy fly, stroke it with greasy fingers and cast it as far as I can. Yes! Another swirl! Another tug on the line! They simply cannot resist this magical find of mine. But I wanted to keep it a secret for now and be the envy of all my friends. I called my creation my *chicken-thigh fly* and I'd win all the competitions if I played it close to my chest.

*

But today was the day my world caved in when I realised my lunch box was missing. With sharp pangs of hunger beginning to strike I considered the options I had. There was a pub up the road I could go to, which meant packing up all my gear. Or I could stay where I was and keep fishing - but probably draw a blank.

It was in this quandary I found myself when my life-saving lunchbox arrived borne down the hillside with waves and shouts by my thoughtful, devoted wife. But when I opened the box and looked inside the whole of my world fell apart. All it contained were strawberry yoghurts, and no sign of my chicken thighs. My wife had picked up a similar box she took to work every week. This was a fishing crisis that demanded immediate action. The solution was simple and quick. We decided to lunch at the local pub and things couldn't have worked out better. She had a small lasagne and I had the last Chicken Special. "And a doggy bag to go with it, please," I said. "Just a small one to dunk a fly in." It was part of my afternoon plan.

*

I was feeling a bit apprehensive as I walked back down to the lake. Without my normal chicken thigh lunch I was certain to draw a blank. Perhaps the doggy bag in my pocket would give me an outside chance. I was tackling up at my favourite spot when another angler walked by, carrying a string of sizeable fish which looked like the six-fish limit. The name on his hat declared he was Sam and he looked the arrogant sort. Even so I tried to be friendly.

"I hope you haven't emptied the place," I said. "It's going to be hard enough as it is without my favourite fly."

When six-limit-Sam asked what it was, I decided to play it real cool. I simply said it caught lots of fish and worked best of an afternoon. He didn't seem too impressed.

"That's no bloomin' good," he muttered, "messing about like that. You wanna get hold of some decent flies if you wanna be catching all day." He opened a gaudy fly box full of equally gaudy lures. "All you need is a couple of these and you'll be catching them twenty-four seven. I tied them at breakfast this morning while making my bacon sandwiches. A smear of fat on your fingers works wonders for most of the day. I call it my *Bacon Fly*." He winked and looked over his shoulder then offered me one to try.

"It's our little secret, eh? If you don't catch the buggers with one of these you might as well call it a day. Pack up. Go home. You don't look the sort for a challenge," he taunted.

Don't look the sort for a challenge! Sam was quite a lot bigger than me so I decided to keep my cool! I was really angry and thoroughly choked with what this monster had said. Worse than that, it seemed my method of catching fish wasn't exclusive to me at all.

Six-limit-Sam had just spoiled that. His jibes made it even worse.

*

A short while later with six fish in the bag I pondered the situation. Three had been caught on Sam's *Bacon Fly* and three on the *Chef's Chicken Special*. But despite the day's unhappy events I wasn't to be put down. This method of using flavoured flies was something that clearly worked, at least for chicken and bacon. There must be some others, too. So yes! I'd show this surly character I could go one better than him. Rather than keep it a secret I'd turn the whole thing around and spread the news of these special flies to the whole of the fly fishing world. And I'd draw up a marketing plan, to sell ready-made full strength flavoured flies of every variety. By Mail Order. Internet. I'd do the lot. I'd put vending machines for flavoured flies in every Fishery car park. I would soon be a millionaire! Feeling a whole lot better I rushed home to draw up my plans. Not fit for a challenge, Sam reckoned? "Right, my fly fishing Bacon Fly friend. We'll jolly well see about that!"

I never saw Sam again. Rumour had it he pushed

his luck when he entered a competition. He overdid the flavouring a bit and a frenzy of fish pulled him in. He very near drowned so they say. Wishful thinking perhaps? I didn't care very much as I sat upstairs in the Boardroom dunking flies in a roast beef gravy. I'm always willing to offer some help when the orders come flooding in. I find it a bit of a challenge!

Thank you, Sam, thank you. I owe my first million to you.

6. ELEVENTH HOUR ENCOUNTER

He knew he was getting forgetful and he'd never done it before but when they said he might end up in prison the reality of it dawned.

"Hello, mister. Our dad goes fishing like you."

I turned around to face a young boy and girl who'd crept up quietly behind me. He was about ten years old with freckles, and was wearing a baseball cap. She was quite a bit older and dressed for a Sunday fete. Their dog, a lovely old Labrador, sat dutifully in-between them. They were presumably brother and sister, and seemed keen to chat for a while. The boy appeared to be spokesman.

"Yes, he does the same sort of fishing that you do. You know, waving your line in the air. Then after a while he lets it go but he's no further out than before.

Daft, that's what I call it, an absolute waste of time. If it were me I'd tie a stone on the end and cast it out in one go. But my sister here is the clever one. She cracked it ages ago."

"You mean casting a line correctly, like you saw me doing just now?"

"Well, she does it like that most of the time – but ties a proper stone on the end!"

A moment of tension hung in the air as they waited for my reaction. Then, unable to contain themselves any longer, they burst into jubilant laughter.

"We're not talking about *real* stones, mister, but stoneflies. They cast really well!"

They chortled with glee at hoodwinking me and sat themselves down on the bank. I could sense I was up against something here but wasn't quite sure what it was. Caution was signalling me.

"So where do you come from?" I asked. "Better still, what are you doing out here?"

"We're staying with granddad," the girl replied, "just a couple of miles away. We like to go out exploring each day and today we've ended up here."

As a granddad myself for several years my protective instincts kicked in. Young folk like these shouldn't wander about in remote places like this. I was worried about their safety.

"Do you think that's a good idea?" I said. "Anyone could be hanging around and you'd have no idea who they were."

The girl nodded towards the dog.

"She'd kill 'em," she said with a confident smile, "with just one snap of the jaws. Instantly, silently, cleanly. It would all be over in seconds. So don't make a sudden movement or there'll be one hell of a mess. By the way, your line's gone all straight."

My line had gone all straight! That meant only one thing to me. A prize-winning trout of wheelbarrow size must have taken my fly. And in spite of the young girl's warning I forgot and leapt to my feet. It was not a good move, I was soon to find out, as the dog was quicker than me. It barked and pinned me down to the ground and started licking my face.

"She's only doing her job," she cried as she attempted to call it off. I somehow managed to delve in by bag and offered it half my lunch. A chicken and mayonnaise sandwich disappeared in less than ten seconds but had the desired result. The girl was full of apologies as she made sure the dog was alright. The day was saved by her brother who deftly landed my fish, and we gathered round to inspect it, dismayed by its miserable size. The children were shaking their heads.

"It could have been one hellava fish if you'd put a stonefly on the end," they agreed.

*

We sat in a row on the bank studiously putting the world to rights as we watched the end of my line. I was curious to know a bit more.

"So what does your granddad do? Perhaps I've seen him around? Does he ever come fishing here it being so close to home?"

"Oh, no," the girl whistled, vigorously shaking her

head. "He hasn't got time for that. He runs the shop in the village with the post office bit at the back and the place was heaving with anglers today buying their annual licence. You know, the one you have to buy every year which allows you to fish everywhere. It's the beginning of April again."

"Licence! Licence! Oh, hell!" I jumped to my feet and ran hot and cold on the spot. In all the years I'd been fishing I'd never forgotten before. It was something you never, *ever* forgot. Unless you had money to burn. It must have been something to do with my age. My consternation was noted with interest by both of my two new friends who seemed to nudge one another and exchange meaningful looks. She discretely winked at her brother who was gravely shaking his head.

"Oh dear, oh dear," the little girl said. "What happens if you get caught? Fishing without a licence is an unforgivable thing. Does it mean that you'll go to prison – or even be shot at dawn?"

I paled. "Well, hopefully nothing as bad as that. But I'll be heavily fined without a doubt, how much I'm not really sure."

"Well, now's your chance to find out," she whispered, staring over my shoulder and giving her brother a kick. "The Environment Agency man's turned up and he's definitely heading this way." She turned to her younger sibling and suggested they make a move.

"Let's get out of here, brother," she urged, "we don't want to get involved. We can't be party to serious crime, not at our tender age."

Without so much as a backward glance they hurried away and a few minutes later were chatting away to the man from the Agency. As the three of them stood in a huddle I wondered what the children were telling the man when they kept on pointing at me. Surely the two weren't welching on me and quietly spilling the beans?

*

Minutes later a shadow fell over me and my forgotten miserable fish, which only served at that moment in time as evidence of my crime. The man was standing beside me, a serious look on his face.

"Morning," he said quietly, glancing down at my fish. "It seems you've been a bit lucky, especially today of all days?"

"Well, with a little imagination I suppose you could say that was true but I'm sure those children have mentioned the gaffe I've made and forgotten to renew my licence. If it's anything in my favour I've never forgotten before. How much is it going to cost me?"

He was grinning and shaking his head. "Just a kind understanding, that's all," and he pointed towards the girl and boy who were watching us from afar. "They've just confessed to winding you up and wanted to say they were sorry. It was simply something they said. You somehow assumed it was April the first and were fishing without a licence, but today is actually the last day of March so the licence you have is still valid right up to midnight tonight. Now, that's something those blighters knew very well but didn't let on for a lark. And as for me being the Agency man, well that's a whole load of twaddle. I'm actually their poor old granddad trying hard to keep up with their pranks."

He pointed across to the opposite bank where the boy and the girl were now standing carefully keeping their distance. "We're really sorry," they called out together. "It's an early April Fools' day prank. We feel wretched for leading you on."

"Yeah, I bet," I replied as I looked across at their innocent, smiling faces.

*

Minutes later I was there on my own, feeling enlightened and rather relieved. I hadn't been fined or gone to jail, or prepared for the firing squad. And I'd had the strangest encounter with two very likeable kids and been privileged to share a few precious hours of their happy and carefree childhood. That was okay by me.

Bemused, happy, and whistling a tune, I carefully tied on a stonefly and quietly carried on fishing.

7. A PISCEAN POINT OF VIEW

A little imagination is needed here as two of our piscean fishing friends observe life from under the surface and make fun of us human being.

Hey, Tommy, look who's arrived!
It's the bloke with the ten-piece rod.
The salesman told him he'd catch more fish
The gullible silly old sod.
It takes him all day to fix it all up
And there's always a bit left over
And his fishing hasn't improved one bit
Although he's had it since last October.

GET HOOKED!

Don't look now but Fatty's turned up
The one that we love to hate,
Just look at the way he's parked his car
He can't even get that straight.
Why can't he park like everyone else
Neat and tidy in just one space?
He certainly thinks he's the Big I Am
And acts like he owns the place.

And have you noticed he's got a new hat
Well, doesn't he look a sight,
With flashing lures pinned all round the brim
He looks like the Northern Lights.
And did you hear what he did at the Game Fair
Well, it really brought tears to my eyes,
He tripped as he entered the portable loo
And lost most of his favourite flies.

Well, who have we here, it's Mary McLaen
I haven't seen her for months
She's clutching a bag of something
I bet it's her husband's lunch
No, it looks like a loaf of wholemeal bread
And she's chucking it everywhere
Oh, the lads are gonna love her for that
In fact - they're gonna go spare.

DAVE REES

Hey, Tommy, the bloke with a limp
Has bought himself a new car
Cor! I bet it cost him a bob or two
Yet it looks a trifle bizarre.
It's nearly all black with a splash of green
Like a giant Montana on wheels
Strewth! I can't believe what I'm seeing
It's got hub caps like fishing reels.

There, he's parked it up by the entrance
On that small piece of sloping ground
He really wants all the world to see.
He's been splashing his money around
But he's waving his arms and running back down
With a worried look in his eyes
Jeez! The silly old fool's left the handbrake off
So...better watch out you guys!

God help us, Tommy, the dog man's turned up
With Fido his four-legged friend
It never stopped barking the last time they came
They drove everyone round the bend
The old boy kept shouting for peace and quiet
And gave him a bone to gnaw
Which shut the dog up for a minute or two
Then it started howling for more.

GET HOOKED!

Hey, would you believe it the bailiff's appeared
And he's got a woman in tow
Just like he had last Thursday
The crafty old so and so
They seem to be having a cuddle
Well, that's what you'd call it I think
And I heard him agree it was okay with him
How many fish she caught - nudge wink.

Well, bless my soul who's this we have here
It's Arthur who's just turned sixty
He's just got back from his birthday fling
Where he consumed vast amounts of whiskey
He apparently had a whale of a time
With some woman from Finisterre
Now he's trying to cast with his arm in a sling
Hmmm...I wonder what happened there.

Well I dunno about you but I'm getting fed up
With this same old crowd all the time
So I reckon it's time we livened things up
With a heart-stopping tug on each line
Make sure you give them a short sharp pull
Make their adrenalin really flow
So... I'll race you round the island and back
Are you ready? Steady? Let's go!

8. BACK TO SCHOOL

He thought he was getting far too old to think about women now but something she said made him change his mind – could she be his catch of the day?

It was The Invitation that did it, or rather some words that were on it. I was cordially invited to go back to school to attend a Reunion Day – the first one they'd ever held. There'd be a welcome drink and a buffet lunch, but it was the offer of fishing that caught my eye. The private lake in my old school's grounds was being opened for fishing that day. It was a chance to recall those happy times spent fishing there as a boy. My RSVP was soon in the post – it was too good a chance to miss!

Reunion Day duly arrived and down at the lake I was just about ready to cast a fly when I heard voices coming toward me. It seemed like a children's nature walk and as voices and laughter got nearer and louder I wondered what best to do – should I stay where I was and carry on casting, or try and keep out of their way? A rather attractive teacher sensed my dilemma and turning to face the children she slowly lifted a hand. The children and voices stopped at once and the more curious ones at the end of the chain strained to see what was holding things up. Then, having captured the children's attention, she spoke for a while about lakeside life while pointing at things around them. Dragonflies, moorhens and swallows all came under close scrutiny. And then she pointed at me.

"This is a fly-fisherman," she announced. "They come in all shapes and sizes but mainly like this one here. They are perfectly harmless creatures usually found lurking by rivers and lakes and invariably coloured green. Sometimes they have a smile on their face. Sometimes they look a bit grim. Perhaps if I asked him nicely he might show us what fly-fishing means?" She raised her eyebrows and faced me with an enquiring look on her face. I was rather bemused by her candid approach and assumed what she meant by this subtle request was to see some action from me. So, what could a fisherman do? I pulled off some line and made a few casts to the sound of appreciative murmurs which turned into gasps of astonishment when I had an immediate take! It had to weigh seven pounds at least and as I carefully played it towards the bank the more they became excited. But there were those that simply covered their eyes as they guessed what might follow next. I needed to check on what to do now and drew the teacher aside.

"What shall I do with it now?" I asked. "I've only two possible options. Dispatch it or let it go."

She looked round at the children's faces then whispered her sound advice.

"I think it best that you let it go or you'll start off a hate campaign."

I netted the fish with care as I wanted to give the children a chance of seeing nature close up. It was a magnificent spotted brownie, the best I had ever seen. The children closed in around me all anxious to have a look and asked lots of questions about the fish and its secret life in the lake. What sort of food does it eat? Where does it sleep at night? Most of them wanted to touch it, others kept well away. After twenty minutes of questions they reluctantly had to leave but not before standing in silence as they watched me setting it free. As they set off again in crocodile file we listened to various comments they made about the demonstration they'd seen.

"I'm gonna fish like that when I'm old."

"And I'm gonna buy a fishing rod and come here every day."

And so it went on. An interest in nature had started to show which would hopefully grow and grow. The teacher was clearly intrigued by it all, and by the seeds of interest I'd sown.

"Thanks for getting involved," she said. "Far better they saw things really close up than me standing and pointing at things. It's something I'll bear in mind."

*

I seized the chance to ask her a question. "Whatever happened to Charlie Brown who was headmaster when I was here? I know that he held the record for the biggest fish ever caught. It tipped the scales at a whopping five pounds and his name appeared on the Honours Board. Well, I caught a seven pound brownie that very same day, just like the one just now, but it didn't count for the Honours Board because of the witness rule. My seven pound catch wasn't witnessed by at least two other people. Only Charlie was with me that day. I was rather miffed at the time but it wouldn't bother me now."

She smiled and held out her hand. "I ought to mention I'm Liza Brown, Charlie Brown's only daughter. Dad has just turned ninety now and I succeeded him as Head of the School. Dad often mentions what happened that year and thinks the rules were unreasonable, too. It should have been you on the Honours Board but as headmaster he had little choice. He had to abide by the rules. But that was then and now is now and we live in a different world. In fact it's a private school for girls and has been for quite some time. The Honours Board disappeared years ago but your catch today was a record and ought to be mentioned somewhere. I'll write a piece for the School Magazine and the school's new website as well. Perhaps you could give me some details? Shall we start with that whopper just now?"

I wasn't too happy with that. "I don't want to be ungrateful but can we give that a miss? I'm not too bothered about glory and fame, and mentions on Honour Boards don't really matter now. Let's just say I've had a great day, I've caught a nice fish, and spent time with some really great kids. But the most rewarding moment of all for me was to see the look on their faces as they watched me setting it free. That moment in time was priceless and worth a thousand mentions to me."

She was nodding in silent agreement. "I couldn't agree with you more. If that's all you want in the glory stakes then fine, that's okay with me." Suddenly, she was nothing but smiles. "Now, what are you like with a wheelchair? You have a driving licence I hope? My father may well be ninety years old but he's made it down to the lakeside where he's waiting to say hello. If you wouldn't mind wheeling him back later on I'll leave the rest of the day to you both. Lots of tight lines and I'll see you later I hope."

*

But it wasn't a chat that he had in mind. It was more like an angling challenge. He suggested we had a fishing match like the last time we fished together, while chatting about old times. It would be a competition between him and me as to who caught the biggest fish.

"Trouble is," he admitted sheepishly, "I think I'm the winner already. I couldn't wait to get going this morning and started fishing without you. Blow me. I caught a beautiful rainbow straight away weighing at least five pounds. It was a really beautiful specimen and just had to let it go. But I managed to get it witnessed first as Fishery Rules require. You haven't forgotten them have you?" He didn't wait for a reply and grinned. "But I doubt if the need will arise. I mean, a five-pounder will take some beating." He joyfully clapped his hands.

I didn't know how to break the news to my ninety-year-old headmaster then remembered this sporting challenge was actually his idea. So, no point in me getting soft-hearted now. We needed to see it through.

"Well, I'm sorry to disappoint you," I said, "but I started without you, too, and netted a beautiful brownie weighing a touch over seven pounds." It was my turn to wear a grin. "Sorry. Seven pounds was the best I could do."

He frowned and scowled at me all in one as his apparent victory seemed in danger of being stolen by me. Then a smile of triumph returned and he waggled a finger at me. "Ah, but did you remember the Witness Rule? You needed two people to witness your catch, just like I had to just now."

I could have easily said I had plenty of those - by way of 24 children and one grown up, namely his daughter Lisa. Beat that! But something was holding me back. Once again it wasn't important to me to claim any sort of a victory. So best let him have his moment. We all needed one now and again. Perhaps this year the need was his. So I lied.

"Oh, damn – I forgot! The witness rule. So victory is yours once again. Now, let's get you back to the school house before I forget where it is."

*

After saying hello to some faces I knew and exchanging a memory or two, I found myself ready to leave for home but Lisa was flagging me down.

"I have something for you," she said. "Something the children have done for you since watching you fishing this morning." She thrust a handful of drawings into my hands with instructions to take them home.

She'd asked the children to draw a picture of what they remembered most of all of their nature walk earlier that morning. As I thumbed through the pictures before me I could see a fish and a fisherman depicted in every one. Not only was I drawn in all shapes and sizes but was invariably coloured green. And the fish that I'd caught was enormous in size and sometimes bigger than me. I was touched and it made my day.

"They're much better than trophies with names on," I said and Lisa nodded agreement. It was then that I spotted the painting on top was different to all the others. It seemed to depict a fisherman and a woman fishing together. I pointed it out to Lisa who, in a matter of just a few hours, was slowly growing on me. I suddenly felt daring and bold with words running wild in my head. I suggested a competition. Just between her and me.

She didn't take long to reply. "That would be nice," she said, "as long as you don't mind losing to someone as hopeless as me. Give me a ring this evening and we'll fix something up for tomorrow."

I was chuffed and bravely rattled on. "There'd be conditions of course. Like insisting I pay for dinner whoever might be the winner. I don't get the chance very often and won't take no for answer."

"It sounds like an offer I can't refuse," she said coyly with a smile. "You've cast out your line and I'm hooked."

*

As I made my way back to the car I felt elated and 20 years younger and started to think of what fly to use in our competition tomorrow. But what the hell did it matter! More important than that was to be with someone I felt comfortable with and share special moments together. Like those special moments this morning when we released that beautiful brownie and watched it gliding away. But should I strike lucky with Lisa no way would I let her go. Because Lisa would be my catch of the day and I'd have a keep net to hand. So, all you other anglers out there wish me luck for tomorrow. You're never too old you know!

9. MONTANA MAN

He could tell by the way they were looking at him that something wasn't quite right. They seemed nervous and apprehensive – was there something they wanted to hide?

It was the time of year that hinted of winter and I waited a while for the mists to clear before venturing down to the lake. Although the sun had risen a while ago, its warmth was still struggling through. But I was in no hurry to fish today. I wanted to get the feel of the place as I'd never fished there before. I was there as a guest of Farmer Grant, who I'd called on the previous day. There was a sizeable man-made lake on his land and he ran a small fishing syndicate that I was rather anxious to join. I explained that I'd moved into the village and was looking for somewhere to fish, and asked if I could take a look at the lake with a view to joining next year. Half an hour later I left with a smile on my face. He'd suggested I go the following day now that the season had finished.

"You're welcome to bring a rod as well as there might be a fish or two. Have a look round and get the feel of the place. You'll have it all to yourself."

How lucky can a fisherman be?

*

As it turned out, I wasn't fishing alone next day. Just one hour into my fishing, a movement caught my eye. It was blue, about five feet tall, and carrying a made up rod. It turned itself into a teenage boy heading slowly in my direction as though he'd be fishing opposite me. I couldn't help feeling a little annoyed as he'd probably get in my way. But my selfish reaction was blown sky high as soon as he started to fish, stripping off line and casting his fly under trees I'd avoid like the plague. All he did then was sit on the bank with a cigarette in his mouth watching every movement I made. Eventually he waved and spoke.

"Morning," he grinned, calling across the water. "I don't think I've seen you before. I hope you don't mind me fishing just here but this is my favourite spot. And now that the season's finished it will be nice to have someone to talk to. Have you got a Montana on?"

Did I have a Montana on! I was surprised how direct his question was coming straight out of the blue. It wasn't a fly I used often and shook my head in reply.

He grinned and stood up again, casting easily under a tree. "Well, that's what you want. Green and black. Then give it a tweak like this." He hardly made a movement and got an immediate take. I couldn't believe what he'd done.

"Come on now," I muttered as he swiftly netted his fish. "That surely must be beginner's luck. It couldn't be anything else."

"Or like this!" he exclaimed a few minutes later when he was into a fish again. "Or like this! Or this! Or this!"

I couldn't believe what was happening. I'd been there for almost an hour before then and never got so much as a touch. Yet in the space of just a few minutes he'd brought five fish to the bank. And he returned every one. He beamed as he wound in his line, carefully placing his Montana fly in a box he took out of his pocket.

"See. I told you to fish a Montana," he said, making a move to go. "I wish I could carry on fishing but I've got to call it a day. I'll be needed up at the church at three and I really mustn't be late. Perhaps I'll see you again. In the meantime, the best of luck with your fishing."

*

As he melted into the distance I decided to finish as well, as I'd already made the decision that, based on the boy's performance, this was the place for me! I made my way up to the farmhouse looking for Farmer Grant as I wanted to talk about membership for the following year. Both he and his wife were at home anxious to know how I'd fared and were pleased when I said I'd like to join the syndicate if I could. Minutes later a Membership Card was mine with Fishery Rules on the back.

"Welcome aboard," he said shaking my hand, "and we hope you'll enjoy it next year. But what was it like at the lake today? You must have found it hard going especially at this time of year?"

"It certainly was for me," I said, "but the boy who was down there with me was having a whale of a time. He must have caught five in all and he wasn't there very long."

They both looked at me rather sharply. "Boy? Did you say boy? So you weren't there just on your own?"

I said no, but sensing the boy was of interest to them I decided to tread with care. Perhaps the boy was a regular poacher, or someone's son from the village. I didn't want to cause any trouble and made a point of adding that the boy had returned them all. But their interest didn't end there.

"What was he wearing, this boy," they asked next, "and what sort of age would he be?"

I said he was wearing blue denim and his age was about sixteen. "He certainly knew about fishing, all he used was a single fly."

They exchanged solemn glances between them and the wife went on to explain.

"Yes, that's why he's known as Montana Man. It's the only fly that he liked to use and, with only pocket money to spend it was the only one he possessed. They say he's often down at the lake but we never go down there now, nor believe in that sort of thing. It brings back such awful memories of the day the poor lad was drowned. He was only nine at the time and was trying to rescue his only fly caught deep on the bed of the lake. Somehow or other the fishing line wound round him several times. My husband tried hard to free him but just couldn't break the line and believes that he comes back to haunt him. He's convinced he's really to blame."

She paused to look at her watch. "Well, we'll say goodbye for the moment as we've got to walk up to the church. His memorial service starts at three and we mustn't be late for that."

"That's just what the boy said" I ventured. "Whose memorial service is it? Is he a local boy?"

"It's for Tom our little Montana Man. Our one and only son. He would have been sixteen years old by now had he still been alive today. Now, if you'll excuse us, we ought to be on our way."

*

I didn't know what to think. I felt confused and my mind was a whirl as I thought back over the day. Did I dream that meeting down at the lake, or was it all very real? I just had to go back to the lake again to where I and the boy had been fishing. Yes, there was the flattened grass where he'd sat, and one or two cigarette ends. And there at my feet was the face of a boy staring up at me through the water.

I shivered and turned away. I didn't believe in that sort of thing. Or should I?

10. FISHING CAN HARM YOUR HEALTH

A strong dislike of health food forces hubby to go it alone. He can't get enough of the wrong sort of stuff until Saturday afternoons.

If you were to ask me what I like most
About bedtime on Friday nights
It's knowing I've got to go fishing next day
It's one of the weekend's highlights!
It's not that I'm a fanatic
I just need my Saturday fix
So I've been lying awake for most of the night
To make sure my alarm rings at six.

DAVE REES

Saturdays are special you see
When we each do our own little thing.
I can go where I like, I can do what I like
And have one helluva fling
I've told the wife I go fishing
But it's more like a food foray
To get some relief from that healthy stuff
She keeps feeding me every day.

The first thing I do when I get downstairs
Is get rid of her healthy food spread
And quietly get the frying pan out
And have a really good fry-up instead.
The next thing I do is creep out to the shed
Where the family freezer is kept
And quietly take out a couple of trout
From the freezer bag marked with an X.

The next thing I do is load up the car
With my gear and the two frozen fish
Not forgetting the lunch she's prepared
Of forbidden food. Oh, how I wish!
I know she means well when she does it
She has only my interest at heart
But yoghurts and raisons and sunflower seeds?
Not to mention cold cauliflower tart!

GET HOOKED!

The first port of call on my fishing day out
Is where they sell beer and snacks
But they only sell beer in packs of twelve
And snacks in jumbo-size sacks
So I'll buy one of each while I'm at it
They should last me the whole afternoon
And, oh, what a joy to have something nice
I don't have to eat with a spoon.

Next on my list is the butcher's shop
Where they sell pies which are simply divine
And I reckon I might just treat myself
As it's my birthday in four month's time
Now, pies need less space than yoghurts
As they sit there in nice crusty rows
So let's get rid of my yoghurty things
And buy a load more of those.

My next port of call is the newspaper shop
Where they sell papers and stationery
And although it's not my intention
I can't help but peep at Page Three
But at ninety years old what's the point of it all
If all I can do is dream.
So I'll pick up a magazine or two
That's all about fishing. Not wishing.

DAVE REES

My last weekly call is on tackle shop Tim
To pay him my weekly due
It's the only way I can buy a nice rod
Without wifey having a clue
It'll take four years of this fishing HP
Before I can take it home
And lie through my teeth whenI tell her
That, sadly, it's only on loan.

I'll spend a few hours by the river then
Watching the squirrels and birds
As they munch my lunch from the Health Food Shop
The wife would be lost for words
So I always sit down and join them
With my food and my magazines
And enjoy my gourmet selection
Hmm...it's really the stuff of dreams.

When I get home and unload the car
I'll proudly show her the fish
But it seems they've defrosted so many times
They're beginning to smell a bit off-ish
The look on her face spelled trouble
When I asked if they looked alright
"Oh yes. I saw you catch them this morning, dear.
You can have them for dinner tonight."

11. TACKLE SHOP TEMPTRESS

She was tall, slender and gorgeous, just like you see in the films but when he reached out to touch her he heard a warning voice in his ear.

It was fate. It was quick. It was love at first sight. Of all the tackle shops in the world I had to walk into hers. I spotted her right away at the other end of the store and although my senses had seen better days I wasn't imagining things. Oh no. She was looking at me in a meaningful way that only we blokes understand. I just couldn't take my eyes off of her...I'm sure you know what I mean. It was a case of instant attraction, just like you see in the films.

She was classy, slender, a vision of grace, more than enough to turn any chap's head. It was one of those magical moments in life that happen from time to time, when common sense gets abandoned and desire takes over instead. I started to dream how sweet life would be just having her by my side and couldn't believe it was happening to me. My God, it felt really great! But I knew I had to be sure about this and not make a fool of myself. I'd been given the glad-eye before in the past and got it hopelessly wrong and although it was worth every penny it cost me an arm and a leg! But the more that I looked the more I was hooked and was falling in love again and found myself planning all sorts of things for some Wonderful Times ahead. My dream world was working overtime and really excelling itself.

But that would be in the future. Right now I had a decision to make that could change the course of my life. So flies, fishing nets, leaders and reels all provided some thinking time as I wandered along the aisles. What was I going to do? What was I going to say? For years I'd hankered for something like this and here was my chance at last. That come-on look was getting hard to resist and one thing was clear in my mind. I simply knew that I wanted her. Badly. Not next month. Or next week. But now.

Right. Decision made. I made up my mind and headed in her direction. Just at that point my mate wandered in wondering what I was up to. I told him of my intentions and brand new life and the look on his face said it all. He thought I'd had one of my turns.

"Are you completely, utterly mad! I can see the obvious attraction but think how your wife will react. She'll strangle you first with your fast-sink line then cast you out till the backing runs out and you'll never be seen again. No, you've got to walk out of here, Tony. Forget it. It's just not for you. Believe me. The dream has to end here."

I was more than just disappointed at his sensible, boring advice and felt the first signs of happiness beginning to slip away. Then, just in time, I remembered the words of a far more sensible friend. *You only ever live once you know and when Happiness comes and knocks on your door just grab it for all its worth.* That friend was clearly much wiser than Ron who'd melted into the background. No way was he getting involved.

*

So, nothing could stop me now and I wasn't to be deterred. I was more than happy to do the deed that would ensure a future together. With only the counter between us now I could almost reach out and touch her. She was just as I knew she would be, an angel sent down from heaven who looked meaningfully into my eyes. She was definitely saying I want you, too. All you need do is ask. Take me away and I'll be yours forever. Believe me...you'll be the envy of all your friends and never regret the day.

For a moment I had fleeting doubts about what I intended to do, but I had to have her at any cost now whatever the outcome might be. A divorce from the wife was a certainty when my traumatic confession was heard. A passing assistant smiled and stopped when she could see the state I was in. It didn't take long to realise the cause and whispered quietly in my ear.

"She'll cost you an arm and a leg, of course, but what does it matter if you get taken to heaven two or three times a week. Go on, I can see you are made for each other."

"So, how much for this piece of heaven?" I asked. "Just out of interest of course."

"What does it matter," she coyly said, "to an appreciative man like you? It is only money after all and look what you get in return. A very desirable companion and the envy of all your friends. Imagine their faces when you arrive at the lake with someone like her by your side. Everyone calls her the Temptress Queen. She's the finest rod in the world."

The finest rod in the world! That's right. I'd seen her before in the magazines and fancied her ever since. Seeing her in the flesh like this was more than a man could stand. And I loved the sexy tattoo on her wrist which said *TemptressQueen 10ft #7*.

"I'll have her whatever it costs," I breathed and offered my credit card. "Just take whatever amount you need and I'll worry about it later." When the price of the rod appeared on her screen I nearly died ten times over. It was flashing and beeping two thousand pounds - the price of reality! I came down to earth with a bump. My dreams of the future and brand new life were slipping away from me. But then, thank heavens and to my relief, my credit card was refused. I'd exceeded its limit by twenty times and it had expired some time ago...just like I would have done if I didn't get out of there fast!

I hurriedly made for the nearest door and heaved a sigh of relief. I'd nearly made a fool of myself and realised how stupid I'd been. My brand new life with the Temptress Queen simply wasn't to be. I'd got the message all wrong again. She'd simply been flirting with me.

*

Ron was waiting outside the shop slowly shaking his

head. He'd seen it and heard it all before at various times in the past. He waggled a finger at me. "When are you going to grow up," he said, "and keep those feet on the ground? How many times have I told you before, you're not a young man anymore? Now that you're in your nineties you need to cool it a bit."

But I still rather fancied the Temptress Queen and looked back over my shoulder to the new life that might have been. Happiness called and knocked on my door but in the end I just blew it. She was too dear. I was too old. And happiness came and went.

12. ONE LAST CAST AND A BOY

He knew it wouldn't be easy but there was something he needed to do. It was then he spotted the teenage boy watching his every move.

He'd never been to the lake this early before but today was a little bit different. It was a once-in-a-lifetime visit and there was something he needed to do. He'd carefully selected the gear he intended to use which included a two-piece rod, a reel to go with it, and an old olive-green line. They were things his father had bought him when he'd first shown an interest in fishing, and he wanted to use them today. They would mark the beginning and end of a lifetime of angling, and all the years in between.

He'd fished here and there over decades but this was the place he loved most, a beautiful lake in a valley, it was a privilege just to be there. As he walked down the path to the lakeside he recalled his very first year and although it was sixty-odd years ago now it was something he'd never forget. As a novice he'd stood for hours in the glaring hot sun without so much as a touch, but his persistence ensured he won in the end and he became extremely proficient. He wrote books, he gave talks, he appeared on TV, and was held in the highest esteem.

He was using the olive-green floating line which caught him his first ever fish and the fly he'd decided to tie on today was large, just like the ones he'd used then. While he mended his line and waited he recalled some glorious times but they became a little bit clouded by the thoughts he'd brought with him today. He'd known for a while that he didn't feel right and everything seemed such an effort but still came as a shock when his doctor told him the heart-stopping news. Just three to six months was all he could hope for, perhaps a little while longer. Live life to the full, his doctor advised, so he decided to fish one more time. It was with thoughts such as these he'd accepted the fact that today was his final visit.

His thoughts turned to his wife Jenny, who'd be sitting at home alone, and remembered the time she went with him once, to give this fishing a try. He'd cast out the line then gave her the rod and showed her how to retrieve. She'd hardly completed a figure-of-eight when the line went taut and a monster leapt into the air. She returned his rod and asked with a smile if it was always as easy as that.

He wanted to keep things simple today using tackle he'd treasured for years, but by mid-afternoon without even a touch he just had to try something else. His patience had finally run out. He quickly tied on his favourite fly – quite a bit smaller to those he used in those earlier years as a novice. He tried different spots and different retrieves but still there was no sign of life. But, as tired as he was, he kept fishing, just as he'd done all those years ago. He couldn't believe it was ending like this. No takes, not even a touch.

*

The extra effort was taking its toll but something urged him to make one more cast then he really would have to leave. He was almost afraid to make that last cast, the very last cast of his life, and when he did all hell broke loose at the end of his line when a fish took hold of his fly. It was a beautiful shining rainbow weighing at least four pounds. He unclipped his well-worn heavy priest to make a speedy dispatch but a moment of doubt came over him as he looked down at the fish in his net. All he could see was a life looking up at him, perfectly still, as though waiting to know its fate. And he found himself thinking it wouldn't be right to dispatch it, at least not today of all days. His own life was slowly running out now, so why should another life, too? He knelt down and quietly said a few words then gently he let it go. As it righted itself and sped away he was aware of a boy on the opposite bank watching his every move. He sat perfectly still, head cupped in his hands, as though he'd been there a while. He was sure he'd seen the young lad before, but never with rod or net. He seemed to enjoy just being there.

*

The walk back to the car wasn't easy. He wanted to look at the lake just one more time before making the final journey home. At the spot where he made that last cast he saw a swirl in the water and caught a glimpse of a fish. For one silly, emotional moment he wanted to think it was the one he'd just caught and the one that he'd just returned. Was it saying... thanks and goodbye?

*

He came back to earth when he realised that someone was by his side. It was the boy he'd seen on the bank just moments before. He wanted to know all about fishing and asked lots of questions about rods and reels and what sort of flies should he buy. They chatted for quite some time and the boy thanked him for his advice. He'd like to know more about tackle and things he said and hoped they would meet up again. Without hesitation or second thoughts he handed the boy his rod and reel, and some other tackle too. He wouldn't need them again, he lied, his arthritis was getting too bad. "Just tell mum and dad it was a present from me, and should they have any queries about it my name and telephone number is written inside the bag," he said. "Goodbye and good luck with your fishing. Just promise you'll give it a try. I shall be watching from time to time to see how you're getting on." The boy couldn't believe his ears, nor could he believe his luck, and a smile broke out on the old man's face as he watched him skipping away. It was a smile of satisfaction borne out of happier days but knew that his father would have approved of the gesture that he had made.

His wife was waiting when he got home anxious to know where he'd been. She was surprised he hadn't brought anything back and he explained why he'd set the fish free. He also mentioned the tackle he'd decided to give to the boy.

"I don't know whether I'll see him again but something inside me tells me it's gone to a very good home. It was written all over his face."

His wife lovingly squeezed his hand.

"I know you'll have made a very good choice. It was a wonderful thing to do."

*

Five months later, in early Spring, a car pulled up at the lake disturbing the quietness of early dawn and the mists swirling around. She sat in the car for a while, deep in thought about things in the past and memories all long held. Then, carrying something small and round, she slowly walked down to the water's edge to a favourite spot she knew well. Kneeling down on the dewy grass she slowly scattered some ashes just where she'd promised she would.

"There. It's the very first day of the season," she whispered, "and you are the first one here. And I want you to do what you always do. I want you to catch one for me."

*

On the way back to the car she passed a young boy and a man she presumed was his father. After chatting a while the boy explained that this was his first time there and the first time he'd ever been fishing. He'd been given the tackle a while ago and had promised to give it a try. It seemed to ring bells with the woman who then spotted her husband's rod and bag which she would have recognised anywhere. She pondered the situation and wasn't sure what to say except to wish them tight lines and lots of luck as they'd got the place to themselves. But she knew that wasn't quite true.

13. BEND IN THE RIVER

When the single toll of the church bell rang out he stopped fishing and stood quite still while rivers of rain diluted the tears that slowly ran down his face.

She stood for a while and watched him fishing, his pale green line snaking effortlessly through the air after a casual flick of the arm. It was a sight that she had never tired of ever since she was a girl. When he realised he wasn't alone, he swiftly but carefully wound in his line and extended a welcoming hand. He was smiling and seemed to know who she was.

"Welcome home, Annie McReady, to the village where you belong. I'm Duncan. Duncan McRae. Your father used to fish here with me right on this bend in the river. It was his favourite place."

That's what she wanted to hear. Something that linked with those times in the past when as a young girl she'd often sat there with her father eating the lunch she'd prepared for them both. She was surprised he knew who she was but news travelled fast in that part of the world and her telephone call to the village hotel had been the talk of the village for days. It was a nostalgic visit, she let it be known, and she needed somewhere to stay. As Duncan found them a place to sit, she was hoping her father's lifelong friend would have lots of memories to recall. She was curious to hear every single one from this man sitting beside her.

*

So this was Duncan McRae. Her father had mentioned him often in the letters he regularly sent and had even enclosed a photo once of the two of them together with fishing rods in their hands. To anyone taking a casual glance you could almost say they were brothers. When her father wrote and said they'd become good friends she was thankful and quite relieved as she hated the thought of him living alone when she took up a new job abroad. That special job in the forces meant she very rarely got home but knowing that Duncan was living nearby gave her some peace of mind. Now, with her early retirement next month she was able to come back to the village she had always pictured as home. She wanted to visit her birthplace again and the village where she grew up and say hello to her father's old friends who knew him before he died. Duncan was first on her list and her first port of call had been the small village shop to enquire as to where Duncan might be. "He'll be down at the bend in the river," they said, "where he fished with your father most days. They were always together and inseparable mates. Duncan was crushed when he died."

They said they remembered her too, as much as they remembered the torrential rain on the day of her father's funeral. To the surprise of all who attended that day, Duncan failed to appear, but they later found out he'd paid his respects in a private and more personal way. He went to the bend in the river to fish alone with thoughts of his very dear friend. When the single toll of the church bell rang out he stopped fishing and bowed his head while cold drops of rain diluted the tears that ran silently down his face. Because of that, and planes that won't wait, she never did meet dad's friend. She had to return that day.

Happily, ten years on, she was in the village again and it seemed very strange and almost unreal to be standing there at her father's old haunt with his very best friend beside her. It also occurred to her that Duncan might have been the very last person he spoke to and she wondered what they could have talked about. It was only a minor detail but she felt she wanted to know. She would ask about that later on when she knew him a little bit better. While they chatted away over coffee, which Duncan produced from a flask, she tried to explain the reasons that had kept her away for so long. When he insisted on letting her share his lunch, which he produced from a large canvas bag, she noticed he'd brought two of most things as though it had all been planned. It must have shown on her face and he laughed.

"They said you'd been asking for me down at the village shop. So I've brought enough for the two of us. And lots of memories as well."

*

She found the next few hours rather pleasant listening to Duncan McRae while enjoying his doorstep sandwiches helped down with his homemade wine. He had a wealth of stories to tell of those missing years with her dad – years she couldn't retrieve now as she listened in silent regret.

He delved back into his bag again and took out a small wooden box. Her father's initials were on the lid and when he gave it to her to hold his voice was soft and sincere.

"He dearly hoped you'd go fishing one day as father and daughter together, but accepted the fact you were still growing up and lipstick, dresses and hairdos took precedence for a while. So he had to put it on hold. Yet he insisted his dream would happen one day – and it would happen right here on the river. So, now that you're here at his favourite spot why not make it happen today? There's a rod already made up for you if you'd like to give it a try, and a couple of special flies in the box that he tied especially for you."

She reflected on all those years ago when she denied her father his wish. Now was the chance to put things right and allow him his lifetime dream. They wouldn't be fishing together of course, but in spirit they'd be very close. So yes, she wanted to give it a try. Duncan looked pleased when she nodded okay and led her down to the river bank where she uttered a silent prayer. "Right, Dad," she whispered softly. "Show me what to do now."

Duncan suggested she fished from the bank. She'd find it a whole lot easier from there, he said, the first time she gave it a try. Then, after a little tuition, she attempted a cast or two and the smile on her face and the thrill of it all increased as her confidence grew. Even he was surprised when a brownie fell to a more adventurous cast and watched with enormous pleasure as she knelt to examine her catch. She marvelled at all its markings and its strength when she played it in and her eyes were glistening with overdue tears as she watched it gliding away. "I'll remember this for a long time," she said, "no wonder Dad loved it so much. My only regret is that he isn't here to see that I kept my promise. I really am sorry, Dad."

She felt a comforting hand on her shoulder. "There's no need for any regret. Your dad will have seen it all. I'm sure he's been with us this afternoon in some spiritual form or other. And that isn't all. He knew you'd come back to fish someday and the rod that you used was your father's rod that he asked me to keep for you. And the flies that you used were ones that he tied before saying goodbye to us all. And he tied them specially for you. He made them from bits of colourful wool from a scarf you knitted him once. You were a young girl at school at the time and he wore it with love and pride. So, you can say you've been fishing together at last – brought together by bits of wool and other things from the past. A promise made and a promise kept. I'm sure that he's happy now."

She was glad she'd met Duncan MacRae. He was just like her father in many ways and even looked like him, too. As for her stay in the village, she felt she was really at home and hoped that her family would feel the same when they arrived in a few days time. She wanted to introduce Duncan to her husband and teenage son. When she told him her son was called

Duncan, too, he was pleased and visibly touched. It was a special request of her father's, she said. He made it a long time ago.

She also had a special request if they made this their future home. Both her husband and son would like to go fishing and could he teach them a thing or two? And perhaps she could learn how to tie a few flies from bits of old coloured wool.

14. THE BRIDGE

He thought he heard voices, children's voices, echoing up from below, just as they used to years ago when he fished there with Jimmy his friend. Where was he now?

It was pure nostalgia I guess but something I couldn't resist. The last time I travelled this quiet road was half a century ago. I would have been walking then with my school friend Jimmy beside me as the other half of our team. Our mission was to apply our skills (such as they were at the age of ten) into catching those tricky customers that lived in the stream near our home. After winding its way through several fields the stream met up with a bank, where with silent swirls it was swallowed up by a pipe that ran under the road. If you slid down the bank to its entrance, the opening was safe and large enough for small boys like us to stand up in. And it echoed whenever you spoke. To casual walkers passing by it was simply an ordinary red brick bridge worth hardly a second glance. To us it became a part of our lives and often our second home. And, as is the way with many young folk, fishing became our passion.

*

Sticklebacks. That's what those tricky chaps were. Loads of the blighters everywhere waiting for us to catch them. But we had to be oh so careful of those vicious, jaw snapping, flesh eating sharks. Piranhas had nothing on them. Well, that's what we used to believe. Would there be any there today, now fifty years later in time? I wanted to take a nostalgic look from the bridge that became our HQ and reflect on how it had been all those years ago. With fishing nets bought from Woolworths, Jimmy and I were a deadly team then, and a jam jar with string tied twice round the neck would be full by the time we were ready to leave. It was then that the traumatic decision arose. Take 'em home or put 'em back now?

Well, we took them all home to begin with where my old tabby cat would be sat at the gate waiting anxiously for our return. We stopped doing that when my father said (with a clip round my ear) all creatures deserved a life and we were to take them back in the morning. Looking back now with the wisdom of years I'd like to think that catch-and-release may well have been born about then - much to my cat's disgust.

I parked and walked to the bridge, now smothered in weeds and dark green grass that grew almost as tall as me. The stream still trickled through but being mid-summer it had little depth and I could hardly expect to see much more than a scattering of water snails. But perhaps I heard something instead? Was it the sound of young boys' voices echoing sharply inside the pipe? As kids we bravely explored it once and frightened ourselves to death when a lorry passed overhead. Now, leaning over the parapet, I shouted a loud hello. Nothing. I shouted again to make sure. Still nothing. Just echoes. I knew in my mind I was just being daft and should face up to reality. It was imagination, I'm sure.

There! Did I see a brief flash of silver below me reflecting the afternoon sun? Was it a cautious stickleback darting from stone to stone? I would have loved to investigate had I been dressed for such an occasion. Sliding down banks wasn't me right then but made me recall those years ago when it was part of our everyday lives and dirt on our shirts and muddy wet socks was almost compulsory. We were young, carefree and happy, and newts, tadpoles and frogspawn were triumphantly carried home where we promised my caring mother we'd return them again tomorrow. Only then would she bring sugar sandwiches and a large jug of ginger beer.

*

Later on there were girls, and the inevitable naturally occurred. They became more appealing than wading in streams and our fishing went to the wall. Weddings came and weddings went and with the passing of time new anglers appeared and forays down to the tackle shop started all over again. The bridge was a natural magnet and I wondered sometimes if it might have been known to other kids over the years. We liked to think it belonged to us and gave it a secret name that even now I cannot disclose for fear of a cut throat and death. But one thing I knew for certain whether known by others or not. They wouldn't have caught as many as us – not in a hundred years.

*

As memories hatched in the warmth of the sun I wondered where Jimmy was now. Did he ever think of this special place and our memorable red brick bridge? Did he ever think of the times we had when two days were never the same? Was Jimmy even alive? Perhaps all those many years ago we should have arranged to meet up again at a memorable place like this. Simply for old times' sake.

*

I sighed and returned to the car recalling more precious boyhood years that stretched all around me for miles. One or two things would be different now and I looked round for signs of change. But all I could see were two small boys peering into a jam jar tied round the neck with string. I knew just what they'd be doing. They'd be deciding the fate of those stickleback fish. Should they *take 'em home or put 'em back now?* Just like we used to do. It was a traumatic decision for two lads to make who may have taken all day to catch them. I wanted to see what the boys did next, but I blinked. And the boys were gone.

Well, better get on I suppose. I was on my way to the tackle shop to pick out a brand new rod, a special gift from the family for those retirement years ahead. But whatever pleasures the new rod would bring they could never quite equal the memories I had of a red brick bridge and a stream. And a jar full of fish, of course.

15. HELLO THE GOLDEN YEARS

He really didn't want to be there in case it happened again but a voice in his head kept urging him on, saying "Try it just one more time."

Sense the new world that awaits you
As that shimmering lake comes in sight
A new fragrance and freshness hangs in the air
Nature was busy last night
Embrace what you see before you
Breathe in that crisp morning air
The lake shows signs of promise today
So draw a blank if you dare.

GET HOOKED!

Feel the sun's warmth as it pierces the mist
Dispersing the cold chill of dawn
Feel its growing warmth on your body
As though you were being reborn.
Hear that thrilling clickety-click
As you pull line off your loaded reel
It signals the start of the challenge to come
And anticipation you feel.

Take heed when your memory reminds you
Of things you've learned in the past
That your chances will never be as good
As when making your very first cast
To the front, to the side, to your left or right
What will your decision be?
You really must make your mind up soon
Your quarry waits patiently.

Well, what sort of fly did you choose?
Was it big? Was it small?
Was it wet or dry?
Does it really matter at all?
When fish are rising all round you
Almost anything goes
There are times when even a bent pin will do
So, are you ready? Let's go.

DAVE REES

Take a slow walk round the lakeside path
And you'll come to your favourite spot
And as hard as you try to walk on for a change
You just can't resist it – and stop
Walter the brownie has lived here for years
Just there where the footpath ends
You've returned him on several occasions
You could say you've become good friends.

But ignore him today and leave him in peace
There'll be others along the way
And the lake is fishing quite well they say
Let's try somewhere different today
How about there on the opposite bank
Where those willow trees hang in the air?
No? You'd rather go back to Walter's place
You feel you'd be happier there?

Now, can you see one showing an interest
That should quell any growing fears
That you might be losing that certain touch
You've acquired over all these years?
So patiently, quietly, keep very still
He'll make a mistake quite soon
And take a swipe at your waiting fly
There !! Now you're over the moon.

GET HOOKED!

Can you feel that powerful rainbow
Tugging hard at the end of your line?
Can you see it thrashing and leaping about?
And you murmur...At last! You're mine.
So savour it, treasure it, this moment in time
To allay all those doubts and fears
And surely dispel any qualms you had
About entering your Golden Years.

Cast your mind back as you're leaving the lake
It's been a very long day
You had quite a few takes as the hours passed by
At last things are going your way!
So quietly reflect as you're leaving
The day is over. You won
Will you come back again tomorrow
Now a new page in life has begun?

Look back when you reach the top of the hill
Shade your eyes from the evening sun
Soon it will blaze like an open fire
Look! The evening rise has begun
So wave cheerio to your friends that remain
As dusk turns to night they will follow
Leaving nature to work on in darkness
Preparing the lake for tomorrow.

Made in the USA
Charleston, SC
19 June 2016